Black Bears

by Marcia S. Freeman

Consulting Editor:
Gail Saunders-Smith, Ph.D.

Consultant:
Don Middleton, Member
International Association for
Bear Research and Management

Pebble Books

an imprint of Capstone Press
Mankato, Minnesota

Pebble Books are published by Capstone Press
1710 Roe Crest Drive, North Mankato, Minnesota 56003.
www.capstonepub.com

 Books published by Capstone Press are manufactured with paper
containing at least 10 percent post-consumer waste.

Library of Congress Cataloging-in-Publication Data
Freeman, Marcia S. (Marcia Freeman), 1937–
    Black bears / by Marcia S. Freeman.
    p. cm.—(Bears)
    Includes bibliographical references and index.
    Summary: Simple text and photographs introduce the appearance, behavior, and habitat of
black bears.
    ISBN-13: 978-0-7368-0096-9 (hardcover)
    ISBN-10: 0-7368-0096-4 (hardcover)
    ISBN-13: 978-0-7368-8097-8 (softcover pbk.)
    ISBN-10: 0-7368-8097-6 (softcover pbk.)
    1. Black bear—Juvenile literature. [Black bear. 2 Bears.] I. Title. II. Series.
QL737.C27F24 1999
599.78′5—dc21   98-18283

Note to Parents and Teachers

Books in this series may be used together in comparative activities to investigate
different types of bears. The series supports the national science education
standards for units on the diversity and unity of animal life. This book describes
and illustrates the appearance and activities of the North American black bear.
The photographs support early readers in understanding the text. The sentence
structures offer subtle challenges. This book introduces early readers to
vocabulary used in this subject area. The vocabulary is defined in the Words to
Know section. Early readers may need assistance in reading some words and in
using the Table of Contents, Words to Know, Read More, Internet Sites, and
Index / Word List sections of the book.

Printed in the United States of America in North Mankato, Minnesota.
022014   007979R

Table of Contents

Black bears have
black or brown fur.

Black bears have
short, curved claws.

Black bears live in forests.

Black bears climb trees.

Black bears dig under logs for food.

Black bears look for bugs.

Black bears look
for berries.

Black bears hibernate during winter.

Black bear cubs
play during spring.

Words to Know

berry—a small fruit found on some bushes or trees

claw—a hard, sharp nail on the foot of an animal

cub—a young bear

curved—bent or curled

forest—a large area covered with trees

fur—the hairy coat of an animal

hibernate—to spend the winter in a deep sleep; black bears hibernate in dens.

Read More

Crewe, Sabrina. *The Bear.* Life Cycles. Austin, Texas: Raintree Steck-Vaughn, 1997.

Helmer, Diana Star. *Black Bears.* Bears of the World. New York: PowerKids Press, 1997.

Holmes, Kevin J. *Bears.* Animals. Mankato, Minn.: Bridgestone Books, 1998.

Internet Sites

FactHound offers a safe, fun way to find Internet sites related to this book. All of the sites on FactHound have been researched by our staff.

Here's all you do:

Visit *www.facthound.com*

FactHound will fetch the best sites for you!

Index/Word List

Word Count: 50
Early-Intervention Level: 7

Editorial Credits
Michelle L. Norstad, editor; Clay Schotzko/Icon Productions, cover designer;
 Sheri Gosewisch, photo researcher

Photo Credits
Dembinsky Photo Assoc. Inc./Bill Lea, 16
Elizabeth DeLaney, 4
John Serrao, 14, 18, 20
Mark Raycroft, cover
Robert McCaw, 1, 6, 8, 10, 12